Best wishes

Sarah   Robin

Foreword

Polo is a game for enthusiasts so it is not surprising that a polo playing member of Toulston Polo Club has the enthusiasm to research in depth and record the history of this club as it celebrates its centenary. Interestingly, we think nowadays that polo has grown, which of course it has since it restarted after the Second World War. Today there are fifty seven clubs in England, Scotland and Wales, but back in 1913 there were about the same number of clubs and they were much more evenly spread over the country and not, as now, focussed mainly in the South. Sadly, shortly after Toulston was formed, the First World War broke out and by December 1914 over seventy polo players had been killed in action and over one hundred and thirty wounded. The next four years claimed many more including some of our best players.

Some of the names of the clubs listed one hundred years ago have been revived, but few have spanned that time in the way Toulston has and the book of course describes the history of how that has happened. I am sure that it has not been without its ups and downs and these have either been excluded or lost in the mists of time; if you find someone who says that his club has not suffered from the politics of polo, then I fear that you have probably found someone who does not tell the whole truth.

Congratulations are due to all those who have contributed to this great achievement and above all to Miss Sarah Lloyd. Writing histories of polo clubs is not a profitable business but rather a labour of love and perhaps Sarah will be rewarded with some chukkas on the Maltese Cat in the afterlife.

D. J. B. Woodd Esq
C. E. O. Hurlingham Polo Association
February 2013

Published by Robin Gallagher
Longley Old Hall, Huddersfield HD5 8LB

First published in Great Britain in 2013
in hardback and paperback

Copyright © The Committee and Members of
The Toulston Polo Club 2013

Sarah Lloyd and Robin Gallagher assert the moral right
to be identified as the authors of this work

ISBN 978-0-9575349-0-2

A CIP catalogue record for this book is available from The British Library

Printed in Great Britain by
Peter Scott Printers, Burnley, Lancashire, BB11 5UB

Designed by The Bigger Boat
www.thebiggerboat.co.uk

Contents

Dedication

I dedicate this book to Mrs Christine Haigh, whose death in 2012 left a void at the heart of the Club and with its members. Throughout my few years at Toulston Polo Club, Christine welcomed me with open arms, and made me feel part of a loving family that is Toulston Polo Club. Christine was one of the warmest, kindest and most selfless people I have ever met, and it is clear to see that all who met her felt the same.

Throughout my research, I came across countless letters from members past and present, and visitors to the club who had written to Christine to thank her for her kindness and the welcoming way she treated them at the Club.

Sarah Lloyd, Halifax
February 2013

Preface

"Let others play at other things,
"The king of games is still the game of kings"

- Inscribed on a stone by the polo ground at Gilgit, Pakistan

The inspiration for this book came from a discussion at the 2012 Annual General Meeting. I volunteered to research the history of the Club with a view to producing a book in time for the centenary in 2013. I would like to thank Jim Haigh and Ralph Day for entrusting me with the task of delving into the history of Toulston Polo Club, its members and its trophies. I little realised the extent of the information available and the considerable help I would receive from past and present members and the public. I interviewed many people in preparing the book and due to the volume of memories and anecdotes, I regret space has not enabled me to include everything. However, I can assure you, all the information I have gathered will reside in the Club archives, possibly to be used for the bi-centenary in 2113!

Of all those who helped me, I wish to thank particularly Mr Hamish Riley-Smith for allowing me access to the diaries, letters and photographs of his grandfather, William Riley-Smith, the founder of Club.

In my few years at the Club, I feel that I have become a member of a very special and close family. There are some wonderful members whom I feel privileged to have met and played with I hope as a reader you will find this as fascinating as I have.

Sarah Lloyd
Halifax
February 2013

The History of Polo

It seems only fitting to mention briefly the origins of the game. Polo is thought to have originated in Persia around the 5th Century BC *(or possibly earlier)*. Over time, the game became popular in other parts of Asia, particularly in the Indian Subcontinent and China, where it was common during the Tang Dynasty *(618-907 AD)*. The first recorded polo match took place in 600 BC when the Turkmens' beat the Persians'.

The early form of the modern game began in what is now the Indian state of Manipur. In Manipur the game was traditionally played with seven a side and on indigenous ponies which were no higher than thirteen hands. There were no goal posts and a score was achieved by hitting the ball out of either end of the field.

It was the British East India Company's intervention in Manipur that helped introduce the game of 'Pulu' to the British settlement at Silchar, in Assam. Here, the first club was established in 1854.

The oldest polo club still in existence is the Calcutta Club, which two British soldiers, Captain Robert Stewart and Major General Joe Shearer, established in 1862. Military officers brought the game back to Britain in the 1860's. Edward Hartopp of the 10th Hussars read an account of a game of "hockey on horseback" in *The Field* magazine, and arranged a match on Hounslow Heath against the 9th Lancers. Other regiments soon took up the game and it became an established sport amongst the cavalry regiments. British forces went on to establish the Malta Polo Club in 1868.

In 1874, the Hurlingham Polo Committee drew up the first set of formal British Rules, many of which still exist today. The first polo match at the Hurlingham Club in London was played in the same year. In 1903 the Committee expanded to include representatives from the Services, the County Polo Association, all three London polo clubs *(Hurlingham, Ranelagh and Roehampton)* and from all polo associations within the Empire. In 1925, the Committee was redesignated as the Hurlingham Polo Association *(HPA)*. Polo stopped at the Club at the beginning of the Second World War and afterwards, the compulsory purchase of its land resulted in the end of polo there.

Following the end of the war, the HPA moved to Cowdray, where matches recommenced in 1952.

British settlers in Argentina started playing polo in the late 1800's. David Anderson Shennan owned Estancia Negretti, located about 100 miles from Buenos Aires. The earliest recorded match in South America took place at Negretti in 1875. The sport spread quickly and in 1892, the River Plate Polo Association was founded and constituted the basis for the current governing body for polo in Argentina. The country has earned the sobriquet "The Mecca for Polo" due to it having the largest number of ten handicap players.

In the USA, the first known polo match took place in 1876 at Dickels Riding Academy on 5th Avenue in New York City. The first club was established at Westchester in the same year. The founding members of American Polo were H.C. Herbert, James Gordon Bennett and August Belmont, who financed the original New York polo grounds.

In 1900, the Summer Olympics included polo for the first time. It remained as part of Olympics up to and including the 1936 Games in Berlin when Argentina triumphed over England in the final with a final score of 11 – 0. When the Games resumed in 1948 in London, polo was no longer an Olympic event.

In 1998, the International Olympic Committee *(IOC)* granted the Federation of International Polo *(FIP)* outright recognition to represent the sport. This means that the FIP and IOC will work closely together for the possible participation of the sport in future Olympic Games.

Today polo is played in over 80 countries worldwide.

The Founding of Toulston Polo Club

William Riley-Smith *(I will refer to him as W.RS from now on)* was born on the 28th November 1890, the son of Henry Herbert Riley-Smith and Annie Heaton *(daughter of Ralph Heaton – proprietor of the Birmingham Mint)*. He lived at Toulston Lodge, just outside Tadcaster with his family. The Lodge had extensive grounds and the present club pitches formed part of the estate to the south of the house.

W.RS was educated at Eton and Trinity College, Cambridge. His father was a proprietor of the John Smith's Tadcaster Brewery Company along with his Uncle Frank, and upon his father's death in 1911, W.RS followed in his footsteps at the Brewery and in 1913, he also became a director.

His father and Uncle Frank had horses and so from an early age, W.RS rode. In his youth during the Easter and summer holidays, he would play polo every day with his father's groom, James Rogers. He even played on his sister's pony at times, without her knowing about it. W.RS said he learned a lot about riding off and hitting the ball during those times.

In his time at Cambridge, W.RS played polo at Beyton in Suffolk with his Uncle Frank who lived at Great Barton Hall, near Bury St Edmunds. Frank supplied him with ponies so that he could play three days a week. He played there until 1910. For the remaining years at Cambridge W.RS played on the University ground at Trumpington, which was located just off Rutherford Road *(this ground remained until the 1970's when it was used for housing)*. In 1912, during his last year at Cambridge, W.RS captained the polo team. He tried his best to keep the polo flag flying at Cambridge, but this got more difficult due to the advent of cars, as people wanted to spend their money on this new form of transport rather than polo. The Royal Agricultural Show used the ground at Trumpington in 1920, but W.RS recalls that when he managed to play there a few years later, he found that the ground was very hard in the summer.

WR-S outside his home of Toulston Lodge.

Being so fond of the game W.RS decided he would have to make his own polo ground at his family home at Toulston. At this time *(1912)*, there were already two polo grounds in the vicinity. Cavalry regiments stationed in York founded the York County Polo Club in 1902 on the Knavesmire, near the racecourse. The Leeds Polo Club, the principal club in the north, had its ground at Alwoodley, some distance from Toulston; W.RS' uncle played there from the late 1890's. The ground had poor drainage, and attempts to solve this failed when excavations found a huge rock beneath the surface, and so polo finished there in 1914. Other northern polo clubs included the Middlewood *(the first Club established)*, the Holderness Club *(Hull)*, Catterick Bridge, Cleveland *(Redcar)* and Harrogate, with both of the latter enjoying only a limited life.

In 1913, after coming down from Cambridge, W.RS came back to Toulston and formed the Toulston Polo Club at his family home of Toulston Lodge. W.RS designed the ground with spectators in mind. He created a raised bank so that everyone had a perfect view of the length of the field and he also boarded the ground. Due to the superiority of Leeds Polo Club at the time, play was only on Mondays and Wednesdays so as not to clash with the playing days over at Alwoodley. In early April of that year, the boards arrived and on Monday the 28th April 1913, the club opened with a "Flourish of Trumpets" with around 18 players and over fifty spectators present. The team colours for Toulston were cream with a cerise band on the body and the sleeves - the same as the W.RS racing silks. The opening day was memorable however, as Roger Lamb had a couple of teeth knocked out and just as play finished the heavens opened. Players on that first day included Eddie Robinson, Dick and Harold Nickols, Roger Lamb, Michael Lupton, Walter Lucy, Eddie Tempest, Herbert Sutton, Geoffrey Cowper, Joe Pickersgill, Kenneth Culbert and, of course, W.RS.

I have found one intriguing Internet reference to polo at Toulston, but so far have found no independent support for it. In 1893 *(three years after W.RS's birth)*, the reference mentions the death of E.M. Phillips whilst playing polo at Toulston Lodge. Phillips was a pupil at Leeds Grammar School, as were W.RS's father and Uncle Frank.

Polo at Toulston in 1914, at a time when boards were in use.

Toulston Between the Wars

An early photo of "Changing Horses" at Clitheroe Polo Club (by kind permission of the Clitheroe Information Centre).

Polo continued at Toulston into 1914. In July of that year, W.RS took a team to Clitheroe, in Lancashire - a beautiful ground with fantastic turf, located on the banks of the Ribble. At this time, there was a terrible slump on the stock market, and one player, Joe Watson, remarked to W.RS that war was imminent, and of course, he was right. Within a week, on 28th July 1914, war broke out. That was the last time polo was played on the ground at Clitheroe. Polo at Toulston also ceased for the duration of WW1.

During the First World War, W.RS served with the Yorkshire Hussars, transferring later to the 13th Hussars, which formed part of the Indian Cavalry Division up to 1916. He was posted to Egypt, and later he went to India. It was here that W.RS came across polo again. He played at Meerut *(the Indian 'home' of the 13th)*, and bought a number of ponies there. W.RS then moved to Muttra, where he was made secretary of the polo club. Whilst there he took a team, "The Muttra Tent Club" *(more noted for hunting boars)*, to play for the Meerut Cup and won it! The winning team was made up of Col Brinton, Leslie Ormerod, Jack Gannon and W.RS.

Polo at Toulston recommenced in 1920, and with the earlier demise of the Leeds Polo Club, play could now be held on Monday, Wednesday and Saturday.

In 1923, W.RS decided that the polo ground needed levelling. Unemployment was high, and he felt the work would help alleviate some of the hardship in the Tadcaster area. It took forty men and a horse called Gamble *(loaned from the brewery)* between six and seven months to complete the work.

Early photo of spectators at the pavilion at Toulston.

The top soil and sub soil were removed and the whole pitch lined with ash from the brewery furnace, which accounts for its good drainage even today. Whilst this work was carried out, the Toulston team played on the "Ings" at Tadcaster.

The Toulston team travelled to play at Manchester, a club founded in 1872 and re-located to Ashley, just south of Altrincham, in Cheshire from 1906. They also played at The Wirral Club, which was founded in 1885. Both grounds were very welcoming and had the greatest respect for each other. According to W.RS Manchester entertained the Toulston players well. W.RS described Oswald Moseley, the manager at Manchester, as "kindness personified" and he said the greatest fun was had at Manchester. One match in particular stood out for W.RS where he said the final score was 19 to Manchester and 1 to Toulston. In 1939 the Manchester, Wirral and Bowdon clubs joined forces, but unfortunately this would be the first and last year of the amalgamation before the Second World War broke out and play ended. However, in 1952, polo was restarted in Cheshire and is still played today at Acton, near Nantwich.

After the new ground was laid out at Toulston, the next twenty years of polo were extremely successful. The season generally started on Easter Tuesday and ran through until just before mid-August *(because W.RS went off grouse shooting!)*. Each year the Club played two tournaments, one in the spring, played in the evening *(as it usually coincided with the York Spring Race meeting)*. The other was held at the end of the season. During these years, W.RS would hold lavish parties at his house during the York spring race meeting.

WR-S by the pavilion at Toulston.

At this time his friend Alfred Munnings, the painter, would stay at Toulston. W.RS commissioned Munnings to paint a portrait of his first wife, Beryl on a horse called Snowflake, and paid the sum of £750. Unfortunately, as with many family portraits, the family sold the painting and replaced it with a replica. The original painting sold at Christies in 2002 for £1.5 million!

In his 1926 painting entitled "W Riley-Smith Esq, Changing Ponies", Munnings shows W.RS and his groom on the polo ground at Toulston. In his autobiography, Munnings says,

"... I am reminded of one more place, called Toulston, where I stayed with a good fellow, a famous brewer - Riley-Smith. Already I am recalling dinner-parties; jolly nights with my host at the pianola - wireless not having quite come into its own in those days. His delight was a game of polo. I painted him on one of his ponies; another pony was in the picture - "Changing Ponies", I think we called it."

The painting sold at Sotheby's in New York in 1982 and since then it has gone to ground.

"W. Riley-Smith Esq Changing Ponies"
© Sir Alfred Munnings Art Museum.

In the mid 1920's Toulston did well holding its own, as handicapping was close. In the interwar years, Toulston won the County Cup twice and the Junior Cup six times. These cups were played for at Ranelagh in Berkshire. In July 1929, W.RS took a team to Ranelagh to play in the County Cup Final. Toulston had a 5 goal handicap, and Ranelagh had a handicap of 16, so Toulston were given an eight goal start. The game was tough, and the final score was Ranelagh 13, Toulston 9.

Cavalry regiments stationed in York often sent teams over to Toulston in between the wars, and the Toulston team played at York; Toulston gained great experience from these matches. One of the best teams at York was the 14th/20th Hussars, and according to W.RS, they were always very welcoming, however, he did not find the Royal Scot Greys so hospitable. The introduction of armoured vehicles and mechanised artillery, that had begun during WW I, reduced the requirement for horses in the Army and this had a knock on effect for those regiments keenest on the game.

The County Association and Polo Rules of 1934 name the clubs in the north of England as York, Toulston, Manchester and Wirral. By 1938, the list of clubs in the north had altered to York, Harrogate, Toulston, Manchester, and Holderness *(the club at Holderness was located near the cricket ground on Anlaby Road, where the stables were located and the ground was used for polo practice)*.

Interestingly, the rulebook contains an article from the national railways about the movement of polo ponies by train. It states that the transportation of ponies is at the owners' risk only. Senders must complete a "Live Stock Consignment Note", obtainable at railway stations. It also mentions that concessionary rates were available for polo ponies conveyed by passenger trains to London to compete in matches and tournaments at Hurlingham, Ranelagh and Roehampton *(the 'London' clubs)*, during the season *(May June and July)*; the locations were treated as one destination.

Early photos of polo ponies being loaded at Tadcaster train station.

As well as travelling all over England playing polo, W.RS even played abroad. In 1935, he saw an advertisement about polo being played in Cannes and he decided to participate. Unfortunately, his first year there was disappointing. He was the only player that turned up, and so, after sending a few frantic wires for more people and ponies, he ended up with twelve ponies and three other players including Mike Moseley. The French scraped a few Cavalry officers together. The event was somewhat different to a Toulston Tournament as the guests included kings, dukes and nobility, and there were more photographers there than players! However, despite this rocky start, W.RS continued to play at Cannes for several years and in 1939 he took a team there which included his son Douglas.

In 1935, Harrogate Corporation introduced polo on 'The Stray' and W.RS played there regularly. In fact, a few cups still played for today at Toulston originated from the Harrogate club. Regular play went very well whilst it lasted, but it came to an end in 1938 partly due to residents complaining about the restrictions to their rights of way through the park.

In August 1958, there was a one-off match held on the South Stray, when the Harrogate Polo Tournament was held there. Toulston played the Bradwell team from Cheshire for the Riley-Smith Trophy. Bradwell won 5-4. The Toulston team included H. H. Robinson of Kirby Moorside, Douglas Brown and George Calvert, aged 65 *(There was another one-off match held in the 1980's for charity organised by Jim Haigh)*.

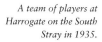

A team of players at Harrogate on the South Stray in 1935.

Of the time in between the wars at Toulston W.RS had this to say:

"The more I look back at those polo days the more amazed I am that we were able to keep things going. It would have been impossible without the greatest and most loyal co-operation of all those stout fellows who gave me their support throughout those years. There must have been times when they went through infinite trouble to turn up at all. We always tried to make our teams as fair as possible and the result was very gratifying in the very close finishes we had to our matches."

When the Second World War broke out in 1939, W.RS had thirty three ponies. The war halted polo not only at Toulston, but throughout the country.

Early photo of a line up, around 1914, Toulston.

Post World War 2

On 1st April 1940 the 518 Field Company, Royal Engineers moved to Toulston Lodge. The following notes come from Richard Hussey's 1994 book "Some Wartime Memories of a Member of R.E.Survey".

"We were rushed up to Tadcaster, Yorkshire, in a mighty hurry. The new billet was the polo stables at Toulston Lodge, owned by one of the Smith brothers of brewing fame. Mind you, it was the grooms' quarters we occupied and did not disturb the horses."

Mr Hussey did well from the transfer, for he married a local girl he met on a blind date!

W.RS said in his memoirs:

"Polo has given me more pleasure than anyone could possibly imagine. I think of all the pleasure I have had from it and hate to think that the war with Germany has cut it off for me in the evening of my career and I shall never hit that wonderful little white ball on the green sward again. I am too old now and so are Charlie, Edgar, Frank and Colonel and Griff, and Tom Paisley, and countless more who made the game so glorious at Toulston."

After the war, Britain was at low ebb, so low in fact that W.RS felt polo would never be played again at Toulston. And so in 1948 W.RS dismantled the ground, took up all the boards and the little pavilion. He gave four ponies away and sold others to Lord Cowdray very cheaply. It was around this time he first thought that Toulston Lodge could be used as a new site for Tadcaster Grammar School. The North Riding County Council eventually compulsory purchased The Lodge in 1948, but the school would only occupy its new site from 1960. However, W.RS retained ownership of the polo ground and from this time, he lived at Toulston Grange, just a few hundred yards from the polo ground, along the A659 towards Tadcaster.

However, despite his pessimism for the future of the game at the time, some polo continued at the club in 1949, 1950 and 1951. W.RS played a little in 1950, but not in 1951, although he watched his friends play with much enthusiasm. One time the Manchester team came over to play and W.RS commented on the match, unfortunately though, apparently half the time the batteries on the microphone were not working!

In 1952, polo restarted officially in England and at this time, the Hurlingham Polo Association was based in Cowdray. W.RS travelled to Argentina by sea this year, but I have no record of what he did there.

In 1954, at the age of sixty four, W.RS died at sea on board the SS Conte Biancanamo on his way to Tenerife. He is buried in the family grave in Newton Kyme churchyard, near Tadcaster. His second wife Ethel Constance Smith died in 1957. After his father's death, Douglas Riley-Smith inherited Toulston Grange and the polo ground, and he too was a keen polo player. Douglas moved to the south of England, playing polo at Cowdray, and was Chairman of the Hurlingham Polo Association from 1974 to 1980. He remained President of Toulston Polo Club until 1979 when he sold his remaining Tadcaster estate, including the polo ground, which he sold to local farmer Douglas Elliott. Mr Elliot rented the ground to the Club for several years. Tony Riley-Smith, W.RS's other son also played polo in his youth, but was less passionate about the game. He continued to live in Tadcaster until his death in 2010.

Painting of The Durham Light Infantry playing at Touslton in 1955.

And so into the 60's

In 1959, Toulston Polo Club had twenty registered members and these included Jim Bell, George Calvert, Milton Asquith, and Tom Blackburn *(names familiar to members today as they donated some of the cups we play for)*. At this time and throughout the 1960's, there were a few stalwart members who ensured the running of the Club went smoothly. These included David Brown, John Hinchliffe, Michael Watson and Henry James Gillam.

In the mid 1960's and 1970's the Toulston Polo ground was used by the Tadcaster community, including the Tadcaster Carnival, and the photograph above shows the John Smith's sports day in 1965.

David Brown was born in 1927 into the engineering family famous for the eponymous tractor business founded by his great grandfather. Later, the family manufactured Aston Martin and Lagonda sports cars. He lived at Meltham, near Huddersfield and kept his horses at his home. David played at Toulston from around 1958 up until 1968. In those early days David's wife would groom for him, and most weeks his son, Adam, would go with him to the ground and watch his father play. David owned on average five ponies, some of which he purchased on trips to Argentina. Adam recalls times he spent at Toulston as a young child when he sometimes sat with the timekeeper, but was never allowed in the pavilion. David and the other Toulston members would often play matches away at places including Cheshire and Cirencester. On many occasions other players from Toulston, including Michael Watson and John Hinchliffe, would, according to Adam, travel back to Meltham after play for wild parties and gatherings. In 1968, David left Toulston and he moved to Buckinghamshire where he went to play at Guards Polo Club, ending up with a handicap of 4!

John Hinchliffe also lived in Huddersfield, in Denby Dale. He played at Toulston from around 1966 until 1976. He ran the family textile business of Z Hinchliffe and Sons Ltd *(today run by his sons)*. He was an integral part of Toulston Polo Club for many years and was Chairman from 1974 until 1976. Looking back at the minutes of the AGM's it is clear to see he had a great passion for the Club and secured its future by recruiting members and followers of the game.

David Brown at Toulston.

John Hinchliffe was not the only dedicated member of Toulston around the early 1970's. Henry James Homfrey Gillam *(the family business was Homfrey Carpets)* was also devoted to Toulston. Major Jim Gillam, as he was known, would often send his gamekeeper, Philip Hayer, to cut the pitch. Jim and his wife Diana Holiday, lived a short distance from Toulston at the 3,000 acre estate of Healaugh. Diana's father was Major Lionel Holliday, one of the most famous racehorse breeders in the 1940's and 1950's, and Diana ran the Tarbrook Stud at Healaugh. Jim was commissioned into the Royal Artillery[1], and often had foreign postings. He was at Toulston from around the mid 1960's and he would often have Argentine players staying over at his house. In 1970 Jim decided that the game was too dangerous for him to continue playing, but he still kept an active role as President of the Club through into the mid 1970's. In 1973 he was appointed High Sheriff of Yorkshire *(he was the last of the High Sheriff's, the title being devolved to the individual Yorkshire counties after 1974)*. In later life, Jim sold 2,800 acres of his estate, and kept 200 acres back on which he built a golf course! He was often remembered for walking around his estate with a cut off polo mallet with a rubber end on it, using it as a walking stick. Major Gillam died in May 2011 at the age of 96.

Michael Watson lived in Bramhope with his sister Lorraine and father Frank. The family owned and ran Farm Shops Ltd, a chain of butchers' shops, together with a small farm. Frank was a keen equestrian and showed horses at many shows, including the Great Yorkshire Show. All three were keen hunters and rode with the Bramham Moor Hunt. Frank, Michael and Lorraine played polo at Toulston from the mid 1950's and Michael continued to play into the late 1960's. He had two children, Gail and Matthew. Gail fondly remembers the times she spent at Toulston as a child watching her father playing. She also recalled that Argentine players would often come over for the summer season, staying with various members of the Club.

Above, Michael Watson (second from the right) and others in the pavilion. Below, David Brown with his son Adam in the early 1960's.

[1] *I did not meet Jim Gillam, but my great uncle, George Haigh, was an officer in the Royal Artillery and after the war he joined Homfrey Carpets as finance director, and often played golf at Healaugh.*

In 1970 Tony Duff was posted to Catterick Camp. As a relation of the Riley-Smith family *(Bill Riley-Smith married his Tony's great aunt)* he knew of Toulston Polo Club and joined. Previously, while at Tidworth he had run Tidworth Polo Club and was on the Hurlingham handicap committee, so knew all aspects of running a polo club. At the time of his arrival at Toulston, the committee members knew most of the rules of the game, but little about the returns and information that Hurlingham required. Although only at Toulston for three years, Tony organised the members. As secretary he took on many jobs including organising the chukkas. He also organised the teams for away matches.

During Tony Duff's time at Toulston, he would travel with other playing members including John Hinchliffe, and Tom Duxbury to away matches at Cheshire, Cirencester and Tidworth. He brought three ponies up from Tidworth and kept them with John Hinchliffe's horses in Denby Dale. Tony had a handicap of 2, having many years experience of the game. He started playing polo on a sand ground in Aden, where many of the ponies were stallions, so riding off involved considerable aggression and bared teeth. This was followed by serious polo in Malaya, playing the Royal houses of Pahang and Johore. After this, he spent two years in Germany playing inter-regimental matches.

One year Tony managed to persuade Jimmy Edwards to come and play at the Toulston Tournament. Jimmy stayed with Tony's sister at Bramham. In return, Jimmy Edwards invited Tony Duff to a show at Billingham that he was doing with Eric Sykes. After the show Tony was invited back stage and he, Jimmy and Eric Sykes went out to supper. He remembers the evening with great fondness, as he spent the whole evening laughing at Eric Sykes ribbing Jimmy Edwards.

At the time of Tony Duff's arrival, membership at the Club was low, and members, including Mr Hinchliffe, were making efforts to promote it. One of which included contacting Lt. Colonel Kishen Singh, who was a serving officer *(and a notable player)* in the Indian Army, having been a member of the winning Indian World Cup Polo Team at Deauville in France. He later earned the prestigious Arjuna award for excellence in polo. John Hinchliffe wrote to Kishen and asked that, if his expenses were paid, would he come over and play? Kishen agreed. Kishen was a competitive polo player who achieved a 5 goal handicap. He played at various clubs in Britain between 1955 and 1975. Colonel Singh played at Toulston in 1974 and 1975 *(after which he went to manage the Ham Polo team in Richmond, Surrey, for three years)*. In his early playing years in England, Kishen played polo with W.RS and later played with Douglas Riley-Smith in the Italian Open in Rome and the Spanish Open in Madrid. Kishen gave Jim Haigh his early polo lessons.

Another past player who was encouraged to join Toulston in the early 1970's was Richard Spilman. He used to hunt, and whilst hunting he met Jim Bell, one of the longest serving players ever at Toulston. Jim asked Richard if he fancied playing polo, as the Club could do with more members.

Richard had ridden horses from an early age on his family farm at Sessay, in Thirsk, and he took to the game well. Jim lent him a pony, and John Hinchliffe lent him another called Pirata. John said he could not get on with it, and so he let Richard keep her in the end. Ian Atkinson, another member, also gave Richard a pony called Doris. Richard recalls warmly the trips to away matches he went on with John Hinchliffe. They would stop at several watering holes on the way and then they would have to play polo when they eventually got to the ground. Richard also had an Argentine player called Santiago Basavilbaso stay with him on occasions over two years, and Santiago invited Richard and his wife Sally over to Argentina. At the height of his playing career, Richard had a handicap of 2. However, in the early 1980's, the first of Richard's three children was born and the demands of fatherhood and greater involvement in the family farming business resulted in him stopping playing in 1989.

One of the more influential members of Toulston was John Nash, who joined in the late 1970's. He had previously lived in East Africa where he managed a 10,000-acre farm on horseback. Whilst in Africa he played rugby, and one time when he was playing a man asked him if he could play polo as they were short of players. He went to the local polo club, and they put him on a high goal pony and told him to let it go where it wanted, and to hit the ball if he got near it! John returned to England in 1970, and it was a few years later that he saw an article in the Yorkshire Post about Toulston Polo Club, and so in 1977 he joined. Later in 1984, at the age of fourteen, John's daughter Cindy joined Toulston and she too played polo for many years. More recently John has become a member of The White Rose Polo Club, but often comes to Toulston to play.

The Calvert Trophy 3rd August 1986, Presented by Christine Haigh.
L to R John Duggleby, John Nash, Justin Gaunt, Richard Spilman, Christine Haigh, Jim Haigh, Cindy Nash,
Beth Barber-Atkinson, Gareth Gaunt, David Keyte.

Jim and Christine Haigh

Jim Haigh M.B.E. was born in 1926 and at one time was a textile lecturer at Huddersfield Polytechnic. He and Christine grew up in Golcar in Huddersfield and they knew each other well for many years before they married in 1960. Together they ran Christine's company F Drake (Fibres) Ltd and received two Queen's Awards for Export Achievement.

In the early years of marriage, Jim and Christine lived at Golcar, close to the business. At one time, the business used horses to move goods between the mills and had stables located close by. In 1968, Jim and the family took a horse-drawn Romany caravan to Ireland on holiday, and this is when Jim's love of horses began. As a result of the trip, Jim ended up buying two ponies, Molly and Yates. Yates turned out to be a terror - he would often rip his bridle off and stamp on peoples' feet as they tried to mount him.

The George Calvert Cup 1981. L to R Ian Atkinson, Jim Haigh, Jim Bell, Ruth Calvert, Josh Haigh, and Tony Keyte.

The Family Tree Cup 10 August 2002. L to R Justine Gaunt, Josh Haigh, John Nash, Cindy Nash, Christine Haigh, Andrew Penty, Diane Garland, Cindy Webster, Melanie Robinson and Andrew Foreman. Front row L to R Gareth Gaunt, Jim Haigh, Ralph Day, Chris Garland and Paul Maxfield Gullett.

Before this, Jim had had little to do with horses apart from hunting on an odd occasion. Jim's doctor told him to take up a hobby, something relaxing like golf, which would give him some exercise. Due to his love of horses, Jim found himself pursuing the game of polo - not exactly golf, and not exactly relaxing either. In 1973, Jim went to Toulston Polo Club and watched the matches. By 1974, Jim had joined the Club, at a time when it was short of players. He bought two ponies, Petra and Chickaleena, and by 1975, he had taken on the responsibilities of treasurer.

The season started in May and continued until early September. Practice chukkas were held on Wednesday evenings with matches being played on some Saturdays and most Sundays, much as they are today. It was also around this time that the bar at the pavilion closed which allowed family members in and around the pavilion for the first time! By 1979, the pony lines moved to their current location.

In the early days, Wilf Robson groomed for Jim, followed by Sue Elliot until February 1977, when Rita Messenger took over the task. Rita still works for Jim and his family and she must be one of the country's longest serving polo grooms. Keeping it in the family, Rita's daughter Val has also worked for Jim for the last ten years, having already spent much of her youth at Toulston. Val's partner is Sebastian Funes, and they have a son Antonio who was born in 2006.

In 1983, Jim and Christine moved their horses to Bowers Hall, Barkisland, where new stables and ancillary buildings enabled better management and training.

During the late 1970's and early 1980's it had become common for the teams to travel far afield; matches were played at other clubs such as Rutland, Cream Gorse *(near Rutland)*, Cheshire, Silver Leys *(based at Bishops Stortford)*, Tidworth, RAF Cranwell in Lincolnshire, and even as far as Scone, near Perth, and Edinburgh, where they would go twice a year. In 1986, Jim and a team played at Ham Polo Club in London. In 1978, the Hurlingham Polo Handicap list had six members listed for Toulston: Ian Atkinson, Jim Bell, Jim Haigh, Richard A. Spilman, Jim Turner and T.A. Turner.

At Silver Leys Polo Club in 1980. L to R the White Team are Jim Haigh, Cliff Urwin, Greg Davies and Richard Spilman.

Members' Cup 1980. L to R Jim Turner, Greg Davies, Josh Haigh, Jim Haigh, John Nash, Cliff Urwin, Dr G Myers, Robert Swires, Ian Atkinson, Ricky Waddington, Richard Spilman, Granville Waddington, and Jim Bell.

In the early years of Jim's membership, the Toulston team was known as the Gymlene Gypsies, and usually comprised Jim himself, John Nash, Jim Turner, Robert Swires and Jim Bell. The Wasps formed another regular team at Toulston with regulars including Ricky Waddington, John Duggleby, Jim Turner, and Justin and Gareth Gaunt. Ricky Waddington's son, Granville, ended up playing at Cowdray Park, and in 1986, he won Best Player of the Year at the Cartier International and received a prize from Diana, Princess of Wales.

Jim recalls affectionately the trips to Tidworth. He went in a team with Major Hugh Dawney, who ran a polo school in Ireland. They usually stayed for five days; the horses were stabled at the Barracks and all the players would stay at the George Hotel nearby in Amesbury. Whilst polo formed an important part of the visit, evening distractions for the players included drinking sessions in the George, and a barbecue at the weekend. Also, the Brigadier held a cocktail party on the Friday night and a ball took place on the Saturday night at Havelock House. In 1989, The Toulston Team won the Tidworth Trophy, which was a fantastic achievement.

Rutland Cup 1989. L to R Malcolm Scholes, Jim Haigh, Sebastian Funes, John Duggleby.

Tidworth Tournament 1989. L to R Lizzie Haigh, Gareth Gaunt, Josh Haigh, Christine Haigh, Jim Haigh, Sebastian Funes and Marianne Gaunt.

In 1977, Jim and Christine still ran F Drake Fibres Ltd. They presented the Silver Jubilee Plate to Toulston, with the intention of using the event to raise money for the Church of England Children's Society. This tournament, formerly known as the Drakes Tournament, is the high spot of the competitive and social year at Toulston. Many hundreds of people attend the Finals Day each year, either in the Club's or the sponsor's marquees. The Tournament runs for three days in June. Club members have a formal dinner on the Saturday and the finals take place on the Sunday. The Church of England Children's Society still benefits from a raffle.

In the 1980's, a friend of Jim's, Arthur Lucas, persuaded Jim to hold a polo match for the charity Riding for the Disabled. Arthur's daughter was disabled, and so he had great affinity for the charity. After some persuasion, Harrogate Corporation agreed the match could be held on The Stray as a one off.

In the Silver Jubilee final of 1990, the Toulston 'Leoline Lions', made up of John Duggleby, Sebastian Funes, and Josh and Jim Haigh, beat the Dalmahoy Team from Edinburgh Polo Club made up of The Earl of Morton, Jeremy Milnes, the Hon James Douglas and Simon Coward. The score was 8 – 5½. The event raised over £17,000, half of which went to Kirkwood Hospice and the other half to the Church of England Children's Society. More recently, in 2011 the event raised over £2,900 for charity.

For a few years during the mid 1970's the comedian Jimmy Edwards commentated at the Silver Jubilee Tournament. Jimmy played at Ham Polo Club. On Jimmy's retirement, his friend Terry Bone took over the commentating, and has done so since then. Terry's career in the Household Cavalry gave him opportunities to enhance his playing skills. He joined the Silver Leys Polo Club at Bishops Stortford playing there for many years and is now President of that club. Established in 1894, it is believed to be the oldest existing polo club in England. Terry played at Toulston during the 1970's. Each year he comes to the Toulston Silver Jubilee Tournament to enthral, and sometimes surprise, the crowd with his unique style of commentating and his detailed knowledge of the game.

As with many playing members in the past, from the early 1980's each year Jim and Christine would often sponsor a player to come over from either Argentina or New Zealand and stay with them from April to September. They would groom and help out with the horses whilst here and play some polo. The players included Sebastian Funes and Santiago Basavilbaso from Argentina, and Greg Davies, Tony Keyte, Baden Broughton *(now Vice President of the New Zealand Polo Association)* from New Zealand. The players would generally be around 2 goal handicap.

When the Riley-Smith family sold the polo ground in 1978, Douglas Elliot, a Tadcaster farmer purchased it. For many years, he rented the ground to the Club, but when he died, the right to buy the land passed to the Samuel Smiths Brewery who purchased it. With the help of Edwin De Lisle, a polo playing friend from Rutland Polo Club, Jim later decided to approach the Brewery about buying the polo ground, and the Brewery agreed to sell. The purchase contact contained a number of restrictive covenants, including that the ground should be used for the sole purpose of playing polo and a ban on erecting any buildings without written approval from the vendor. Jim was able to purchase the ground in 1991 securing the future of the Club. In the first year of ownership, Jim wasted no time in creating a second polo ground on the top side of the original ground. In late 1991, the ground was dug up, top soil and sub soil removed and the drains put in. Then, in September, with the soil replaced, the seed was sown. A year later in September 1992, the ground was fit for play!

Over the years polo has continued with great success at Toulston, especially since the introduction of the second pitch. Jim continued to play polo until the age of 81, which is a great achievement. Jim has also been Chairman of the HPA Finance and Grants committee since 1994. In May 2012, Jim was awarded a Lifetime Achievement award by the Hurlingham Polo Association.

The Calvert Trophy. Back row L to R, Grenville Waddington, Martin Fewster, Jim Turner, Ruth Calvert, Ricky Waddington, John Nash, Jim Bell,? Front row L to R, Justin Gaunt, Jim Haigh, Gareth Gaunt, Richard Spilman, Robert Swires, Josh Haigh, Paddy McIldowie.

Terry Bone.

As with any club over the years, people come and go. I am aware of many members who, whilst at Toulston, made a big impression on the Club devoting lots of their time to both the game and the Club. More recently, the Foreman family played at Toulston. Their enthusiasm for the game led them to set up a polo club in Beverley in 2002. Hedley Aylott started playing polo at Beverley and he too was smitten by the bug and in 2007, he formed the White Rose Polo Club located in North Cliffe on the outskirts of Beverley. In 2005, Paul Piddington formed the Vale of York Polo Club located near Bawtry, Doncaster. These clubs have helped to promote polo in the North of England and, together with Toulston, provide healthy competition for the game both regionally and nationally.

Family Tree 1998.

A quiet moment, Jim and Christine at Toulston in between chukkas.

DLI Trophy 2000 presented by Nellie (Marriane Gaunt's mum).
L to R, Duncan Sharp, Johnny Abraham, Jim Haigh, Josh Haigh, Peter Emmerson, Kevin Peschke, Gareth Gaunt
and Ralph Day.

Sir Walter Gilby Trophy 22 July 2000, presented by Reenie Buchanan.
L to R, Ralph Day, Mel Robinson, Glynis Shaw, Jim Haigh, Josh Haigh, Reenie Buchanan, Peter Emmerson,
Cindy Webster, Diane Garland, Justin Gaunt.

Terry Bone and Jim Haigh at the Silver Jubilee with Josh Haigh's son Alex practicing stick and ball.

Family Tree 19th August 2012.

Behind the Scenes

There are many people, past and present, who make Toulston Polo Club special. I mentioned before, at one time only players could use the pavilion - no one else was allowed. In the early days membership of the Club was by the personal invitation of W.RS. Jim Bell, one of the longest playing members, recalled to Jim Haigh that he received an invitation from W.RS to play at Toulston. Also Richard Spilman recalled in his early years at Toulston there was a steward at the pavilion and players did not pay for their drinks during the season, but would settle up their bar bill at the end of the season, some sooner than others!

But on the arrival of Jim and Christine in the mid 1970's, things changed quickly. About this time the bar in the pavilion closed, the pony lines were moved and all were welcome in the pavilion. These were big changes and players today may find it difficult to imagine the Club with strict demarcation lines between players, grooms and spectators.

Soon after her arrival, Christine organised tea and cakes after the match on Sundays, and this change was much welcomed by the players. The tradition continues today. Each week players and their families bring food to share, and there is something for everyone. Ralph Day's burnt Lincolnshire sausages are legendary! Christine's home baking was always superb. I must say, it is a welcome and relaxing time after charging round the polo ground for an hour!

Toulston Polo Club is one of the best examples of a club that is run by its members for its members. Over the years, there have been many players and their families who have devoted a great deal of their time to the club in various ways. These people, some of which do not play polo, but for whom without their help, the club would not survive. These include Charlotte Dennis who for over twenty years has looked after the timekeeping and scoring with great accuracy, and helps with the teas, along with any other jobs that need doing. More recently, Robin Gallagher has helped Charlotte.

Charlotte Dennis and Robin Gallagher with Lizzie on Comma.

Charlotte Dennis and Ralph Day.

Robin and Marianne Gaunt with Sarah Lloyd.

Robin Gaunt timekeeping in the pavilion

From 1979, Marianne and Robin Gaunt acted as a backup team to Toulston and to Gareth's and Justin's polo activities. Marianne did the truck driving and grooming either at Toulston or at the Quorn Pony Club in Rutland at weekends or holidays. For more than fifteen years, Robin organised a barbecue at their home in Sicklinghall on the Saturday evening of the F Drake Silver Jubilee Tournament. Each player contributed and two or three lambs were roasted Argentine style and were enjoyed by up to seventy people. Hospitality was given to visiting team members who came to stay, with their ponies, grooms, children and dogs. Both helped with the running of the club, time keeping, teas, and functions.

Melanie Robinson is a long-standing member, having played polo avidly for over ten years, until she finished playing around 2007 to look after her young daughter, Ruby. This does not deter Mel for attending Toulston most weeks to help in any way she can, including the tea duty. Mel also organises the Friends of Toulston Polo Club, which involves selling Club merchandise.

We all miss Christine Haigh for many reasons, not just for her baking and teas. My mother, Christine Gallagher, has made the tea duties a labour of love and each Sunday makes sure there is tea for all after the game. Not only does Christine make the drinks (a task that sounds simple in itself for those unfamiliar with the set up in the pavilion) but she also looks after the housekeeping of the club, cleaning, and washing. This is as well as warming up and cooling down my pony in between chukkas.

Centre: Christine Gallagher, with L to R Howard Hall, Sarah Lloyd, August Atkinson, Stephen Fall, Andrew Penty, Lizzie Haigh and Josh Haigh.

Tom Blackburn Trophy, May 2011. Meg presenting the Trophy. L to R Howard Hall, Rita Messenger, Beth Barber-Atkinson, Ralph Day, Meg Abu Hamdan, Josh Haigh, Sarah Lloyd, Andrew Penty, Karen Ford, Ray Bull and Julie Fieldsend.

Toulston has one of the most picturesque settings of any polo club in the country.

Another area of the club that requires regular maintenance is the grounds. As I mentioned, Mr Turner looked after the grounds during the late 1960's and into the early 1970's. John Nash also devoted many hours of his time on the upkeep of the grounds during his time at Toulston. He cut, rolled and lined the pitches regularly on the little old tractor, which still sits in the shed today.

More recently, the local farmer Richard Elliot has taken over cutting the grounds. In addition to this, Stephen Fall and Andrew Penty roll the pitches, and Andrew does the lines, as he is rather good at getting them straight!

All members, past and present, have given their time generously to share the responsibilities for running the Club, and it is these people we have to thank for the Club's continuing success.

Toulston Trophies

The inscriptions and names written on the Club's many trophies give an insight into its history and the notable players who have participated at Toulston. Unfortunately, the origins of some of the trophies remain unknown, but the research for this book has uncovered long forgotten information that has helped to take the knowledge further. Toulston won a number of trophies at Harrogate Polo Club, and retained them when it closed in 1938. Prominent amongst these is the Sir Walter Gilbey Cup.

The Russell Allen Cup - 1906
(The Manchester Polo Challenge Cup)

Mr and Mrs Russell-Allen presented this Cup to Manchester Polo Club in 1906. Following the amalgamation of that club in 1939, the Toulston and Cheshire clubs have played for it. No date is set for the matches. Traditionally, the losers of the previous game must challenge the cup holders to play. Games can take place twice a year. Toulston won the Cup in 1999 and in 2005, Cheshire won in 2006 and Toulston has not issued a challenge since. Perhaps in our centenary year we shall see the challenge become an annual event.

The Russell Allen Cup.

Gaunt Trophy - 1925 and 1996

W.RS presented this trophy in 1925 for the winning team of the Junior County Cup in the Northern Division of the County Polo Association. Toulston, Cheshire and the Wirral often played for the cup. In 1925, Wirral won the cup with a team made up of W. Paul, G.G. Lockett, P.D. Holt, and R.K. Lockett. Like the Cesarewitch Cup, this Cup also went missing for a number of years. Then, in 1995 it came up for sale at Hartley's Auctioneers in Ilkley. The highest bid came from the Gaunt family in what Gareth described as a nerve racking auction. Robin, Marianne, Gareth, and Justin Gaunt presented the cup to the Club and it now bears their name.

The Gaunt Trophy.

Cesarewitch Trophy - 1928

The name Cesarewitch is an anglicized version of "Tsesarevich", the title of the heir to the throne in Imperial Russia. There is a flat horse race held at Newmarket called the Cesarewitch, which started in 1839. This race honours the Tsesarevich Alexander *(later Tsar Alexander II)* for his donation of £300 to the Jockey Club *(a sizable amount at that time)*. Unfortunately, not much more is known about the origins of this little cup. It went missing a number of years ago but then in 2001 Mr Tony Long, a member of Rutland Polo Club, presented it to Toulston. Apparently there was some connection in the past with Tony's wife and the nearby Newton Kyme Estate in Tadcaster *(formerly a long time seat of the Fairfax family)*.

The Cesarewitch Trophy.

Tom Blackburn
Challenge Cup - 1930

Tom Blackburn was born in 1909. He lived and farmed at Fogerthorpe near Selby and hunted from an early age and played polo at Toulston during the interwar years. Tom most probably presented the cup to the Harrogate Polo Club in the 1930's. When that club closed in 1938, the cup found its way to Toulston. In the late 1950's, an Argentine team won the cup and thinking it was theirs to keep, took it back to Argentina. Unfortunately, it has not been seen since! The Cup played for today is a replica, which was first played for in 1962.

The Tom Blackburn Challenge Cup.

The Members' Cup - 1936

This is the most magnificent cup in the Toulston collection. It is a close replica of a cup in the Burrell Collection in Glasgow. The Club members presented the cup to W.RS on 18th November 1936. In 1937, the winning team comprised T.W. Worsnop, C. Brownless, W.S. Griffiths and Edgar A. Swift.

The Members' Cup.

Sir Walter Gilbey
Trophy - 1937

This trophy originated with the Harrogate Polo Club. Toulston won it in 1938 and kept it after the Harrogate club closed that year.

Above: Sir Walter Gilby presenting another Trophy at the Harrogate Polo ground in 1936.

Adjacent: The Sir Walter Gilby Trophy.

Durham Light Infantry Challenge Cup - 1956

(see page 14)

The Durham Light Infantry presented this trophy to the Club in 1956. On the evening of 24th August 1955, after York Races, the 1st and 2nd Battalions of the Regiment played a match at Toulston. The Regiment had an excellent reputation for polo going back to the early days of the game. Remarkably, this match was the only time the battalions played against each other. The 2nd Battalion won 7 goals to 1. Lionel Edwards produced a painting of this match. The DLI Journal reported on the match and thanked the Club for providing all the ponies. The Regiment gave a new trophy to the Club the following year.

The Durham Light Infantry Challenge Cup.

George Calvert
Trophy - 1965

George Calvert was in his thirties when he joined Toulston in 1934 and he remained an active playing member until 1964. W.RS said that 'he went into the game with great zest'. George lived with his wife, Ruth, in Beckwithshaw, just outside of Harrogate. George supplied food products to catering businesses. He also bred ponies on his farm. When George died, his ashes were scattered on the pitch at the Club. Annabel Everett is Ruth's Goddaughter and, whenever she can, she presents the trophy to the winning team. When Annabel cannot make it, her grandmother, Ellen-Ruth Einhorn, does the honours in her stead.

Jim Haigh and Annabel Everett with the George Calvert trophy.

The Milton Asquith Memorial Trophy - 1979

Milton Asquith was a former player at Toulston in the early 1970's. Eileen Asquith presented this trophy in memory of her father, who enjoyed watching polo at Toulston in his nineties.

The Milton Asquith Trophy.

Silver Jubilee
Plate - 1977

Jim and Christine Haigh presented this plate to the Club in honour of the Queen's Silver Jubilee. In its first year Jim's team, the Gymlene Gypsies, lost to the Scottish team Dalmahoy. They have returned each year to play at the Silver Jubilee Tournament, and to revisit friends and enjoy the competition. This tournament is the highlight of the polo season at Toulston.

The Silver Jubilee Plate.

Tadcaster Carnival Cup - 1977

Toulston allowed the use of its grounds for the Tadcaster Carnival for several years. In gratitude, the Tadcaster Carnival Committee presented the Club with this trophy, which was first played for in 1977.

The Tadcaster Carnival Cup.

The Haigh Family Tree Trophy - 1983

Christine Haigh and Jilly Emmerson *(whose family played at the Guards Polo Club)* presented this Cup to the Club. In the early days, the Cup was played for not only at Toulston, but also at Rutland, Tidworth and Culverthorpe Hall near Grantham, where the Emmerson's lived. One year Mark and his sister Emma Tomlinson played for the Cup, and won. Another year Satnam Dhillon and his father Kuldip Singh Dhillon also played for the family Tree Trophy.

The Haigh Family Tree Trophy.

R G Curtis Memorial
Plate - 1992

Adam Pappworth presented the plate as a memorial for his parents. The Cup is awarded at the Silver Jubilee Tournament to the best turned out Toulston pony.

The R G Curtis Memorial Plate.

The Spring Cup - 1993 and the Border Fame Cup - 1993

The Spring cup was presented by Peter Emmerson and the Border Fame trophy presented by Judy Emmerson.

The Spring Cup.

The Border Fame Cup.

V E Plate - 1995 and the V J Plate - 1995

Christine Haigh presented these plates to commemorate the 50th anniversaries of the end of the Second World War in Europe and the Far East.

The V E Plate.

The V J Plate.

The Barkisland
Ladies Plate - 1998

Diana Haigh, Josh's wife, presented this plate.

The Barkisland Ladies Plate.

Jim Bell Plate - 2002

Mrs Elizabeth Bell presented this plate in memory of her husband, Jim Bell, who died in 2002. Jim farmed at Grafton in North Yorkshire and W.RS invited him to join the Club. Jim played at Toulston from 1952 until 1999, retiring from playing at the age of 83 - the longest playing member of the Club by far. Jim provided the passion and enthusiasm for the game that helped the Club survive during the difficult years of the 1970's and 1980's. Jim bred ponies and brought them on, and if anyone wanted to try out polo, he would always give encouragement and advice, and often lent them a pony. As the last member to wear a pith helmet and breeches, he was a memorable player at Toulston. He had a handicap of 0, always played Number 4 *(defence)* and never missed the ball!

Christine Haigh and Elizabeth Bell with the Jim Bell Plate.

Jim and Christine Bell at Toulston.

The Odgen of Harrogate Armada Dish - 2005

One of the more recent additions to the Toulston Polo Club Trophy collection is the Ogden of Harrogate Armada Dish. This Dish is played for as part of the Toulston's premier polo weekend in June; the Silver Jubilee Tournament. The tournament has been sponsored by luxury jewellers Ogden of Harrogate Ltd since 2005.

Summit celebrate polo success, winning the Ogden of Harrogate Armada Dish.
Left to right: Hedley Aylott, Howard Hall, Suzanna Ogden, Tony Wesche and Matt Pinney.

The Summer Cup - 2006

This lovely Cut Glass Vase was presented by Toulston members in 2006. Unfortunately, due to bad weather, the Vase has not been played for in the past two years.

Howard Hall with the Summer Cup.

Current Playing Members Stories

August Atkinson

August was born in 1991, and is studying veterinary medicine at Bristol University. August arrived at Toulston in 2008 with her mother, Beth, and began playing by borrowing a pony from Jim Haigh. Rita, Jim's groom, showed her the ropes and in 2010 August got her first pony, acquiring a second in 2011. Having passed her HGV licence recently, August now plays polo regularly at Toulston, by herself or with her mother. She captained the University team in 2011.

Beth Atkinson-Barber

Born in 1960 Beth is a director of a shipping business and began riding from an early age. Beth met Jim Haigh when riding to hounds with the Rockwood Harriers; she was nineteen and living in Shepley with her parents. Due to lameness in her horse, she decided to try polo instead. Through Jim, she got to know Jim Turner, a polo player who was just about to give up the game, and Beth ended up buying her first two ponies from him. John Nash kindly took these ponies and got them fit for her. The first time she got on one pony, she went over backwards and landed in a muckheap! Beth then started playing at Toulston and she, and Cindy Nash were the only female players there. Both she and Cindy played at the very first ladies tournament held at Ascot Park Polo Club. When she was twenty seven, Beth married and moved away from the area. However, in 2008 she returned to Toulston and played regularly. Beth said that, in addition to the beauty of the ground, the great thing about playing at Toulston is everyone gets to play, and no one is left out.

Ray Bull

Ray was born in 1956 and lives in Gainsborough. Ray was friends with Alison Nichols, Ralph Day's first groom, and through her met Ralph. Until recently, his experience of horses had comprised about six lessons as a child. Ray started coming to Toulston with Ralph in 2009, and he rode a little and stick and balled. In 2010, he bought his first pony, Misty, has recently acquired another youngster and is now a regular playing member of the Club.

Richard Clark

Born in 1977 Richard works in commercial property. He lives near Selby, and has four ponies. Richard has ridden all his life and was a member of the Vale of York Pony Club. His mother and father taught him to ride, as they both have a passion for horses. Richard started playing polo whilst at Reading University, and later joined the Ham Polo Club. Richard's job brought him back up to Yorkshire in 2004 and it was then that he joined Toulston. He travels to Argentina on occasion and plays with the Talamoni family whom he has known for years. Richard's highlight at Toulston was winning the Silver Jubilee Plate with Tim Rose, Tom Colie and Henrie Brown in 2009.

Ralph Day

Born in 1953, Ralph lives at Redbourne in North Lincolnshire. Ralph started riding at the age of twenty six, and joined the Burton Hunt. According to Ralph, the hunt welcomed novice riders and had the added attraction of having some young ladies who stylishly rode side-saddle. Ralph soon found that riding was a good way of keeping fit, and wasn't too painful *(as long as he did not fall off!)*. And so, as well as chasing a fox in winter, he thought he could chase a ball in summer, and play polo. Knowing little about the game, Ralph drove to Windsor, followed the signs directing traffic to polo, and watched a match in Windsor Great Park. The programme contained an advert for polo lessons, which he replied to several weeks later and after a two-hour session, Ralph was hooked. From there, he went to Ireland and made several trips to Argentina.

Initially Ralph joined Rutland Polo Club, and acquired two ponies, Romeo and Willow. Around 1989 he joined Toulston. On one memorable occasion when umpiring at the Silver Jubilee Tournament, Ralph fell off his pony - it wasn't even moving at the time! He hoped no one had noticed as he was at the far side of the ground. However, Terry Bone, the outspoken commentator, made sure everyone knew what had happened! Although Toulston is some distance from his home, Ralph plays regularly at the Club.

Samantha Fairbank

Living in Harrogate, Samantha was born in 1978, and is working for a telecoms company as a project manager. Samantha started learning to ride at the age of four. In 2008, Samantha had a taster polo session at the White Rose Polo Club and enjoyed it so much, she continued to play and so joined that club. After learning the game, Samantha bought her first pony, Herbie, in May 2011; a pony that used to belong to Andrew Penty. In 2012, Samantha came to Toulston, as the Club is nearer to her home and, like many, she said she was attracted by the beautiful setting of the ground and the family friendly atmosphere of the members.

Stephen Fall

Born in 1963, Stephen runs the family farm near Thirsk. The family all rode from an early age and his brother, Alan, who has played in the south for twenty years, currently plays at the Guards Polo Club. Over the years, when visiting his brother, Stephen would stick and ball Alan's ponies until, one year when Stephen arrived, Alan said, "Get on, today you are playing."

One game later and he was bitten by the bug. After a lesson with Josh, Stephen's wife Louise suggested trying his mother's retired hunter, Angel, and after practicing with a tennis ball and a broom shaft in the paddock at home, Stephen turned up again at Toulston to play. Someone was heard to ask, "Who is that farmer who comes in hunting gear?" After eight years, he now has six ponies, a groom and a Shetland for his children to practice on. Welcome to polo, it's a highly addictive sport!

Julie Fieldsend

Julie was born in 1970, and lives in Redbourne. She was brought up on a farm and from an early age rode her friend's pony, or fell off her friend's pony - eleven times, she fell off in one day! Anyway, after a while Julie got her balance and started riding other ponies. After school Julie worked at a riding school and whilst there, her friend Ruth told her she knew someone who wanted a groom. That someone was Ray Bull, who was asking on behalf of Ralph Day. And so Julie, at the age of nineteen, went to work for Ralph. For the last thirteen years, her loyal companion, Buster, her four-legged friend, has accompanied her to Toulston; the dog meets and greats everyone who arrive at the Club. Although Julie knew nothing about grooming or polo when she started, she learned fast and now is one of the most knowledgeable people at the Club and always ready to help or give advice.

Gareth Gaunt

Gareth was born in 1968 and he and his brother, Justin, learned to ride in France at a young age. In 1979, one of the Toulston players introduced them to the game. They were soon allowed to join in club matches and became valuable members in both home and away teams, playing mainly Scottish clubs, Rutland, Cheshire, Tidworth and Silver Leys. They were members of the Quorn Pony Club's Polo teams in Rutland becoming the British champions in 1988. Gareth is an equine vet and now runs the family farm, Carlshead Farms, with its diverse activities. Justin left England at seventeen to pursue an international polo career and has attained a handicap of 5.

Paul Maxfield Gullett

Born in 1955, Paul lives in Lincolnshire with his wife, Lesley. He was introduced to the game whilst grooming for a friend in 1990. Since then he has played in clubs around the UK and in Kenya and Sweden. Paul was the polo manager and chief umpire at Rutland Polo Club, and is currently the chief umpire and a coach at Leadenham Polo Club. He joined Toulston about ten years ago but before this, he played in tournaments here and helped to win the Silver Jubilee Tournament one year. In addition to being a HPA instructor for the last seven years, he is a C grade umpire.

Lesley Maxfield Gullett

Born in 1954, Lesley lives in Lincolnshire. Lesley had ridden for many years, producing show hunters before taking up polo. Now an established player, she often travels to Argentina and plays polo near Córdoba. She joined Toulston ten years ago and also plays at Leadenham Polo Club and runs club games at the Rutland Polo Club. Lesley and her husband love to come to Toulston and often make the 200 mile round trip. Lesley was vice-chairperson of the International Women's Polo Association when it started in 1997.

Elizabeth Haigh

Lizzie was born in 1967. Being Jim's daughter, polo became a major part of Lizzie's childhood. From nine years of age, she would go with the family to Toulston every weekend and to other clubs for away matches. Lizzie rode a little and as a teenager she joined in the odd chukka; however, her older brother Josh would constantly ride her off!

Lizzie's studies and job have taken her to London, Canada and elsewhere, and so she spent a lot of time away from Toulston. More recently, Lizzie has worked in York and in 2008 this brought her back to Toulston. Lizzie spent time on her own riding and practicing stick and balling. From 2009, Lizzie has been a regular player and tea maid at Toulston. Lizzie had another break in 2011/12 when she spent a year sailing round the world in the Clipper Race. Back with polo, she found her sea legs worked wonders for her game.

Josh Haigh

Born in 1964, Josh joined in the family love of polo and the Toulston ground at an early age and even time away at school did not dampen his enthusiasm for the game. Josh started riding around the age of fourteen, and joined in chukkas shortly after. At the age of sixteen, he started playing full time. By 1982 Josh had become a full playing member of the Gymlene Gypsies *(which later became the Leolene Lions)*.

In November 1984, Josh went to New Zealand for six months and spent the time travelling and playing polo whenever he could. Josh recalls one memorable time when he played in a seven-goal match for Waimai. The team included three 0 goal players, Josh, Jamie Douglas and Granville Waddington; the fourth playing member was Tony Devitch (NZ), who was a 7 goal player!

Josh stands out on the pitch by wearing a motorbike helmet. He explained to me that one year, his horse spooked and he came off. His hat was just knocked off his head as he landed and ever since then, he prefers the increased safety of his helmet instead.

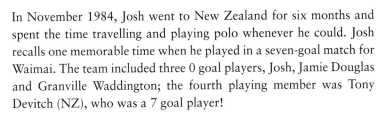

Howard Hall

Howard was born in 1964, and is a technology entrepreneur. Howard lives between homes near Cawood and a small village close to Cardiff. Whilst living at Ledston Hall near Castleford, his neighbours ran the nearby Ledston Hall Riding School. Howard would read *Horse and Hound* each week, and eventually the "Learn to Play Polo" advert tempted him to book a week course at Ascot Park Polo Club. Having never ridden before, he crammed in as many riding lessons as possible into the two weeks before his trip there.

The course in August 1994 gave Howard the polo bug and in the following year he travelled to New Orleans and played there for a few weeks with friends from Ascot Park. On his return, Howard bought two ponies and by the 1996 season his polo activities had grown to having an 8 goal team, and employing three professional players who played all over the country. Since then Howard's polo activities have not been as glamorous, but he has managed to continue to play overseas with occasional trips to Argentina and Dubai. After many years of trying, in 2010 Howard and his team won Toulston's main competition, the Silver Jubilee Tournament, which Howard says was one of his best polo experiences. Howard has been a regular member of Toulston since 1999. He has one task for organising club chukkas each week, having mastered a system for quickly doing the chukka board.

Jane Horner

Born in Essex in 1973, Jane Horner moved north for university, met and married a Yorkshire man and now lives in Blackwoods, Easingwold with her husband and daughter. Jane enjoyed horse riding as a child, but this took second place to swimming, at which she competed at national level. She only took up riding again in 1999 when she bought an ex-point to point horse. Then, in 2002, when Jane's parents moved to Sotogrande in Spain *(renowned for golf and world class polo)*, she decided to take up polo. The elements of pace, skill and athleticism of the horses and riders and the competitive nature of the game together made it an extremely desirable activity. Moreover, the opportunity to meet new friends and play in a team encouraged her to take the game seriously. Jane started her polo career at Beverley Polo Club and has also played at the White Rose Polo Club. John Nash invited Jane to play at Toulston in 2004 and she continues to enjoy the friendly atmosphere, fun chukkas and fast Sunday Cups here. She has two ponies 'Mr Prom' and 'Evita'.

Sarah Lloyd

Sarah was born in 1979, and rode from an early age. Her mother, Christine, had taught horse riding for many years and had a riding school in Halifax. However, from the age of about fifteen, Sarah had a break from the activity, as her mother stopped teaching. At about twenty five, Sarah took an interest in playing polo and her mother suggested she should speak to Carole Taylor *(a former pupil)*, who has a stable yard at Gildersome in Leeds. Carole's partner, Alberto Barberini, an Argentinian, has spent all of his life in polo. They let Sarah ride their ponies and taught her the rudiments of the game and she bought her own pony, 'Quarta' in August 2008. In 2009, Sarah contacted Jim Haigh and arrived at the club for the first day of the season. She played in the chukkas that day and has attended regularly since then.

Her highlight at the club so far is playing in the Toulston team for the 2011 White Rose Tournament, together with Karen Ford, Stephen Fall and Andrew Penty; it felt an honour to be asked to join a team.

RitaMessenger
See Jim and Christine Haigh Chapter

Rachel Oddie

Rachel was born in 1977, and she runs a business in Pontefract supplying horse equipment. Her family have always ridden and her mother evented and hunted and so it was inevitable that from an early age Rachel rode. In her late twenties, Rachel saw an advert for a polo taster session organised by the Yorkshire Young Farmers Club, and after attending this she was hooked. Rachel then took lessons, and within two months, she had bought her first polo pony. As a competitive player, Rachel plays at various clubs, but says that she loves to play at Toulston. As a child, Rachel's mother, Elizabeth, remembers going to Toulston with her father, who was a local businessman and he went regularly as a spectator and to meet fellow businessmen.

Andrew Penty

Andrew was born in 1953. Originally from Acomb, Andrew now lives in Oulston, Easingwold, and works as a grain/seed merchant. Over the years Andrew has participated in many sports, including hunting, skiing, cycling and hockey. Whilst playing hockey he thought he would try something new, and in 1993 he came to Toulston. John Nash kindly leant him a pony to have a go, and that was it - he was hooked! By 1994 Andrew had bought his first pony, 'Trumpetta', and he asked Meg, a long standing friend to groom for him. Meg said he turned up one day with a big blue Bedford lorry and said "Can you drive this?" to which Meg said "I don't know". Not knowing much about polo, Meg acquired a picture of a pony, and learnt to tack up by looking at the picture. Andrew has bought a number of ponies over the years, including 'Annie', 'Suzie', and 'Minnie' of course who was a fantastic pony *(sadly passed)*. Currently his favourite ponies are 'Panash' and 'Jack'.

Current Members 2013

August Atkinson	-2
Beth Atkinson	-2
Raymond Bull	-2
Richard Clark	1
Ralph Day	0
Samantha Fairbank	-2
Stephen Fall	-1
Julie Fieldsend	-1
Gareth Gaunt	1
Elizabeth Haigh	-2
Joshua Haigh	1
Jim Haigh MBE	-1
Howard Hall	0
Jane Horner	-2
Sarah Lloyd	-2
Lesley Maxfield Gullet	-1
Paul Maxfield Gullett	0
Rita Messenger	-2
Rachel Oddie	-1
Andrew Penty	0

Authors' Acknowledgements

We wish to thank everyone who has helped us in the writing the book. We have received so much information about the Club that it became impossible to include it all. It has been a heart-warming experience to realise so many people hold the Club in high regard. All members and Friends have contributed and they are named in the book. We hope we have included below everyone else who has helped us compile the book, and we apologise most sincerely for anyone we have omitted.

Thanks first of all to Hamish Riley-Smith, for allowing access to the Memoirs of William Riley-Smith and other family documents. Without access to this historical gold mine the book would never have seen the light of day. We also thank him for the use of the photos on pages 5 - 8 and 12.

The Tadcaster Historical Society gave considerable help and support throughout the research for the book. The Tadcaster Community Group Archive provided the photographs of loading the horses on the trains in Tadcaster *(page 10)*. Clitheroe Tourist Information Centre provided the photograph of Clitheroe Polo Club *(page 7)*. Tim Hardy kindly gave permission for us to use his photo of the Ogden Armada Dish presentation *(page 46)*.

We have used an image of the painting "W Riley-Smith Esq Changing Ponies" *(page 9)* by courtesy of Felix Rosenstiel's Widow & Son Ltd of London, © Sir Alred Munnings Art Museum. We thank Emily Bergland of Sothebys, New York, for granting permission to use the photograph of the painting. Our thanks go to Major Chris Lawton of The Rifles, at Durham, for permission to use the image of "1st and 2nd Bn Durham Light Infantry – Toulston – 24 August 1955" *(page 14)*, and for the historical information he provided. Jayne Lownsbrough of the Yorkshire Post kindly gave permission for us to use Ernest Forbes' drawing "Toulston Park" *(front cover)*.

The following helped by giving us anecdotes, photographs, allowing access to documents or carrying out research: Adam Brown, Gale Dale, Tony Duff, Marian and Robin Gaunt, Jim Haigh, John Nash, Richard Spilman, Trevor Atkinson, Andrew Broadbent, Sir Gareth Gilbey Bt, Walter Gilbey, Neil Hargreaves of Leeds Grammar School and Harshwardhan Singh.

We appreciate the assistance given to us in the design and production of the book by: Julia Ford, Douglas Main, Laurence Scott, Kendal Leask, Ralph Day, Howard Hall and Jim and Josh Haigh for additional research and proof reading.

Biographies

Sarah Lloyd

Born in Huddersfield, and now lives in Halifax. Sarah graduated in Law and Accountancy at Huddersfield University. She is a qualified Independent Financial Advisor and works in Bradford for the West Yorkshire Pension Fund. Christine, her mother, taught riding and so Sarah's interest in horse started at a very early age. She joined Toulston Polo Club in 2009.

Robin Gallagher

Robin's family moved from North Wales to Manchester when he was seven. He qualified as a Chartered Accountant and moved to Yorkshire. He had no particular interest in horses until his stepdaughter, Sarah, decided to play polo. Now Robin helps with timekeeping and scoring at Toulston.